NECESSITY NEVER MADE A GOOD BARGAIN.

NO BETTER RELATION THAN A PRUDENT AND FAITHFUL FRIEND.

CREDITORS HAVE BETTER MEMORIES THAN DEBTORS.

HE THAT SPEAKS MUCH, IS MUCH MISTAKEN.

THE WORST WHEEL OF THE CART MAKES THE MOST NOISE.

LEARN OF THE SKILFUL: HE THAT TEACHES HIMSELF, HATH A FOOL FOR HIS MASTER.

WINK AT SMALL FAULTS; REMEMBER THOU HAST GREAT ONES.

IT IS BETTER TO TAKE MANY INJURIES THAN TO GIVE ONE.

THERE'S NONE DECEIVED BUT HE THAT TRUSTS.

BLAME-ALL AND PRAISE-ALL ARE TWO BLOCKHEADS.

FORTUNATE THE MAN WHO LEARNS CAUTION FROM THE PERILS OF OTHERS.

NONE PREACHES BETTER THAN THE ANT, AND SHE SAYS NOTHING.

HEAR NO ILL OF A FRIEND, NOR SPEAK ANY OF AN ENEMY.

SIN IS NOT HURTFUL BECAUSE IT IS FORBIDDEN BUT IT IS FORBIDDEN BECAUSE IT'S HURTFUL.

BE ALWAYS ASHAM'D TO CATCH THY SELF IDLE.

A SLEEPING FOX
CATCHES NO POULTRY.

⊹ ROBERT BYRD ⊹

ELECTRIC BEN

The AMAZING LIFE and TIMES of
⊹ BENJAMIN FRANKLIN ⊹

DIAL BOOKS FOR YOUNG READERS An imprint of Penguin Group (USA) Inc.

FREEDOM LIBERTY

B. FRANKLIN, PRINTER

A BOY ABOUT TEN YEARS OLD was swimming in a pond in early colonial Massachusetts. He was a strong swimmer, and after a while he floated on his back, looking up at the sky. Thick clouds glided by overhead and seabirds soared on the swiftly moving air currents. He swam to the shore's edge and picked up a kite he had left there, and waded back in the water until he stood waist deep. He turned on his back and let out the string, and the kite began to rise. He held on tightly to the stick, and the kite began to pull him along. As he was swept over the pond's surface his startled companions ran along the water's edge, cheering him on.

This was the first, but certainly not the last, time that Benjamin Franklin would amaze his friends with the help of a kite. In fact, Franklin's whole life was amazing. He excelled in many different fields, and pursued the unknown and attempted to understand it.

When we picture Franklin, we don't see the curious, strong-willed boy; we see a bald man with spectacles, already on in years. There is something about Franklin that makes us feel we somehow know him, so unlike the other Founding Fathers peering sternly at us from their solemn portraits. We even affectionately call him Ben.

This perception has a solid foundation. Ben Franklin was not born into the upper classes.

In fact, he rose from the humblest origins to become one of the greatly respected founders of the new nation.

Even so, throughout his legendary life, he often signed his name simply B. Franklin, Printer, displaying the great pride he took in his trade. But he was also one of the most farsighted of the early leaders, possessing a brilliant, questioning mind. And he was driven to achieve success in a remarkable variety of enterprises—as a scientist, writer, inventor, philosopher, publisher, and statesman. He was the perfect representative of the new and expanding nation when he went to the courts of Europe. During his life, he was the most well-known American in the world, a real celebrity of his time.

Franklin believed in moving forward, working hard, and saving to gather wealth. His principle of looking for opportunity and taking it was the same as the new nation's. Only in this fresh and fertile environment could Franklin's ideas come about. His thoughts and actions parallel the growth of America. Here, he believed, anything could be accomplished. He was the proof of that.

Benjamin Franklin was able to envision what his country could become, built on the strength of a thriving middle class. He symbolized in his lifetime, as well as ours, the driving spirit of its people.

BENJAMIN FRANKLIN was born on a snowy day in the city of Boston, on January 17, 1706. Boston was in what was then called the Massachusetts Bay Colony, one of the thirteen original British ruled colonies. Boston was the largest city, the most important port, and the center of commerce and culture in the colonies.

Ships from all over the world docked in Boston's bustling harbor, loaded with tools, fabric, and goods not available in the New World. Some ships carried slaves. Ships from the colonies sent lumber, farm produce, and animal skins back to England and other foreign lands. Ships went to different ports in the colonies, too, such as Philadelphia and Charleston.

Josiah Franklin, Benjamin's father, was born in Northamptonshire, England. He was a religious man but did not believe in many of the teachings of the established churches in England. In 1683, he left with his family hoping to find a place where he could worship freely in America. The Franklins sailed to Boston and moved into a house on Milk Street.

Benjamin grew up there in a crowded household. The Franklins had fourteen children. Benjamin was the youngest boy.

Large families like the Franklins were common

The Franklins arrive in the New World.

then and considered necessary for economic reasons. Children supplied free labor, so almost all except the youngest did some kind of work, helping on farms or in family shops with simple chores. Boys helped their tradesmen fathers carry products and unload wagons. Girls helped take care of the home, washing, serving, cleaning, and caring for younger sisters and brothers. Due to disease and poor living conditions, little more than half of these children survived to become adults.

Josiah had been a cloth dyer in England, but there was little need for colorful textiles in Boston. Most people in Boston were Puritans, and they wore clothes of somber colors. So Josiah became a chandler, one who makes candles and soap. He set up shop in the house with Abiah and their fourteen children. Life may have been hectic, but apparently pleasant. Ben's sister Jane, his favorite of all his brothers and sisters, wrote a letter to him many years later recalling their childhood. "All was harmony," she said.

LEFT: *Benjamin Franklin's house on Milk Street. Other streets in Boston were named Beer Lane, Frogg Lane, Flownder Lane, Cow Lane, Crabb Lane, Turn Again Alley, Sliding Alley, Crooked Street, and Rope Walk. These quaint spellings reflect the style of written English at the time.*

THE PURITANS, who settled Boston, believed that everyone should be able to read the Bible. Most towns in Massachusetts had schools with teachers and books. When Benjamin Franklin was born, most children there were better read than those who lived in London and Paris.

Benjamin was reading the Bible at the age of five. He also read a book called *Pilgrim's Progress*, which was the story of a man's struggle to overcome problems and achieve success through hard work. It made an early impression on him as to how he might live his life.

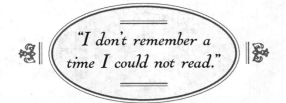

"I don't remember a time I could not read."

His parents recognized his intelligence and zest for learning and sent him to the Boston Latin School when he was eight. They hoped he would go on to Harvard University and become a minister. Ben did well at school, and he was outgoing, popular, and a natural leader. But his independence and dislike for authority ruled out any career in the church. So his father sent him to public school for one more year.

Benjamin began working in his father's soap and candle shop when he was ten. Ben hated the work. The smell of lye and boiling fat sickened

A.

In his father's soap and candle shop, Ben cut candlewicks, poured melted wax into molds, and made deliveries. There were no laws to protect children from dangerous work or long hours.

him, and he found making candle molds boring. He continued to read whenever he could, buying and borrowing books.

"I dislike the Trade," he later wrote, "and had a strong Inclination for the Sea." Ben's father panicked at the thought of him becoming a sailor. One of his older sons had been lost at sea. So he

Some children were taught reading, writing, and arithmetic at home. Children at school used handheld boards called "horn books." They were made of slate and leather and contained lessons and alphabets printed on paper covered with a thin layer of horn.

Philadelphia, the City of Brotherly Love, was founded by the Quaker William Penn. The name is derived from the Greek words philos "love," and adelphos "brother." It expresses Quaker religious tolerance.

FRANKLIN'S LANDING in Philadelphia was less than spectacular. His clothes were dirty and wrinkled, his pockets were stuffed with shirts and stockings. He knew no one, and only had about one dollar. He bought three puffy rolls and walked down Market Street, eating one, with the other two under his arms. He passed the house of Deborah Read, who would become his wife. He later wrote that she "thought I made as I certainly did a most awkward ridiculous Appearance."

Three days later Ben met Samuel Keimer, who was opening a print shop. Keimer was an eccen-

and worked to develop a style of writing like theirs. He secretly began to write made-up letters to the *Courant* signed by a simple country widow he called Silence Dogood, which he slipped under the door of the shop. They became the most popular and anticipated item the paper printed.

Dogood mocked Boston society and its puritanical ways. But the thoughts expressed were Ben's. She championed women's right to education and criticized everything from bad poetry and fashion to Harvard students:

§|| *SILENCE DOGOOD* ||§

I am . . . *a mortal Enemy to arbitrary Government and unlimited Power. I am naturally very jealous for the Rights and Liberties of my Country: and the least appearance of Incroachment of those invaluable Priviledges is apt to make my Blood boil exceedingly . . .*

Sir, Your Friend and Humble Servant,
Silence Dogood

James was furious and embarrassed when the true author of the letters was revealed. His sixteen-year-old brother had established himself as a real voice, a forerunner of a new American form of writing.

In 1723, James Franklin got thrown in jail for publishing opinions that had gone too far. So Ben took charge and published the paper under his own name. He promised he would tone down the writing that made people so angry. At age seventeen Benjamin Franklin found himself the youngest printer, publisher, and editor in all of Colonial America. This lasted for three weeks. When James was freed, he forced Ben to become an apprentice again. He refused to accept Ben as a writer and an equal.

Ben worked hard and knew the newspaper business well. But the troubles between the two brothers grew. James ensured that no other printer in Boston would hire his brother. Ben wrote that his brother's harsh treatment "demeaned me too much." But he also noted that "I had already made myself a little obnoxious to the governing party."

It was time to move on. Ben sold his books to pay for passage and, fearing James might try to stop him, he secretly sailed first to New York, then to Philadelphia. On September 30, 1723, Benjamin Franklin arrived in Philadelphia, ready to start his new life.

BELOW: *Ben sailed from Boston to New York, a city smaller than Boston, without a bookstore or newspaper. It only had one printer, who advised Ben to go to Philadelphia to find work. The entire journey from Boston to Philadelphia took Ben eight days, traveling first by boat, then by coach, and on foot.*

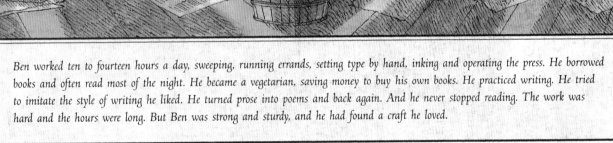

Ben worked ten to fourteen hours a day, sweeping, running errands, setting type by hand, inking and operating the press. He borrowed books and often read most of the night. He became a vegetarian, saving money to buy his own books. He practiced writing. He tried to imitate the style of writing he liked. He turned prose into poems and back again. And he never stopped reading. The work was hard and the hours were long. But Ben was strong and sturdy, and he had found a craft he loved.

AT AGE TWELVE, Ben became an apprentice to his brother James, a printer. Ben wasn't thrilled about the apprenticeship that would last nine long years. But the trade offered him something quite appealing. He would be able to read, write, and edit the printed word.

The apprenticeship did not go well. The two brothers did not like each other and quarreled constantly. Ben learned the trade quickly but James treated him poorly, even beating him when they argued. James was jealous of his brother's intellect, and he considered Ben arrogant.

James was an important printer in Boston. He

> "... all the little money that came into my hands was laid out in books."

published his own paper, the *New England Courant*. The *Courant* was unlike any other newspaper. It was biting, fresh, and controversial. It published articles making fun of politicians, and sarcastic poems, some even written by Ben.

Many of the letters from readers published in the *Courant* were actually written by James's young friends, and they lampooned upper-class Bostonians. The letters were extremely popular with the public, and were signed with such made-up names as Ichabod Henroost, Abigail Afterwit, Tabitha Talkative, and Fanny Mournful.

Ben was anxious to be included in this group

began taking Ben through the streets of Boston to watch the tradesmen work. Cobblers, blacksmiths, cutters, carpenters, wheelwrights, joiners, coopers, and ship builders—all these craftsmen were called the Leather Apron Men because they wore leather aprons when they worked. Ben would always hold these artisans in high regard. They worked hard and were very skilled.

After a brief try as a cutler, one who makes and sharpens knives, Josiah Franklin decided that Ben should enter the printing profession. Ben always considered himself a Leather Apron Man. "Keep thy shop and thy shop will keep thee," he later wrote.

ABOVE: *A. Tavern Keeper, B. Potter, C. Wheelwright, D. Blacksmith.*

BELOW: *Ben's father presided over lively dinner conversations that often included well-informed guests especially invited to broaden his children's minds. Ben professed that he became so engrossed in these talks he lost all interest in food, declaring he could scarcely recall what he had eaten an hour after dinner, and that this "perfect inattention" to food served him well in life.*

Despite claims of "taking little or no notice" of food, he curiously recorded many classic French and American recipes in his memoirs.

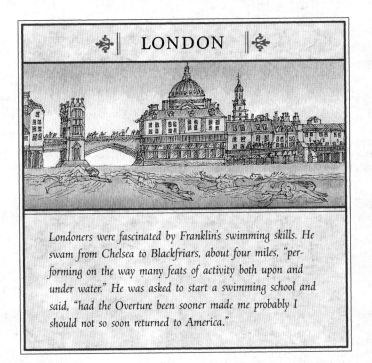

Londoners were fascinated by Franklin's swimming skills. He swam from Chelsea to Blackfriars, about four miles, "performing on the way many feats of activity both upon and under water." He was asked to start a swimming school and said, "had the Overture been sooner made me probably I should not so soon returned to America."

tric, disheveled man who knew little about the art of printing, and was impressed with Ben's craft and immediately hired him as his pressman.

Ben's skills as a printer and writer caught the attention of Pennsylvania's governor, William Keith. He offered to help Ben open his own shop. Ben sailed to Boston to ask his father for a loan, which he refused, advising Ben to go back to Philadelphia, work hard, and save money. While he was in Boston Ben visited James, who was still angry over his running away. He also felt Ben insulted him when he showed up at James's shop wearing fancy clothes and showing off gold coins and a new watch.

When Ben returned to Philadelphia, Governor Keith said he would pay for the equipment for Ben's print shop. So Ben sailed to London in 1724 to buy a press and type. When no money arrived from America, Ben found work as a printer. In 1726 he returned to Philadelphia, and reluctantly went back to work for Keimer.

Back home, Ben was busy with his work, his writing, his interests, and his friends. In 1727 Ben founded a club with some like-minded men, whose purpose was to improve society. To join, members had to take an oath to love mankind. First called the Leather Apron Club, it later became known as the Junto (which in Spanish means together). The club met every Friday night and lasted almost forty years.

Philadelphia, with its central location, was growing quickly as new arrivals landed at its port. It was the right place for Ben.

———————— ✿ ————————

BELOW: *The voyage back to Philadelphia took eighty-three days, which was unusually long. Ben kept a diary, noting the activities of dolphins, sharks, flying fish, seabirds, and even seaweed. He wrote "a regular plan for life," vowing to work hard and save money, to be honest, and to "speak ill of no man whatever."*

———————— ✿ ————————

BELOW: *At their meetings, members of the Junto argued and conducted debates "in the sincere spirit of Enquiry after Truth." Every three months each man had to "produce and read an Essay of his own Writing on any Subject he pleased," which was then discussed by all. They analyzed questions such as: "Is it justifiable for the subject of a king to resist if his rights were taken away?" "Can man arrive at perfection in his life?"*

*B*EN BECAME SUPERVISOR of Keimer's print shop. He ran the press and trained four young printers. When Keimer cut his pay, Ben quit, taking with him one of the men, Hugh Meredith. They borrowed money from Hugh's father and set up their own shop. Ben made the business successful and then bought his partner out.

Keimer owned a newspaper, too, the *Pennsylvania Gazette*. It was not doing well. Seizing his opportunity, Ben began writing sarcastic letters critical of Keimer, which were published in Philadelphia's other paper. He signed them "the Busy Body." These letters helped the *Gazette* fail, and Keimer sold the paper to Ben for almost nothing.

Franklin was the first American to make his own metal type.

"The sleeping fox catches no poultry."

At the age of twenty-two Franklin owned his own print shop and the *Pennsylvania Gazette*, which he soon turned into the most successful newspaper in America. It would make him a wealthy man and a prominent force in the affairs of Philadelphia.

On September 1, 1730, Ben married Deborah Read, the young woman who found his first appearance in Philadelphia so entertaining. He had proposed to her before his London trip, but her mother thought they were too young. Despite only writing to her once from England, Ben noted that when he returned, "Our mutual affection was revived."

Franklin said, "She was as much disposed to industry and frugality as myself," and so the perfect mate. She kept his books and ran a store in the print shop which sold coffee, tea, stationery and ink, and other goods.

As an editor, Franklin was interested in stories that were humorous and that poked fun at

In 1731, there were no bookstores in the colonies. Books were a rare commodity and most of them were shipped from England. Franklin proposed a lending club where all Junto members pooled their books together. The group formed the Library Company of Philadelphia, America's first library. Any citizen could read books at the club, but only members could check books out.

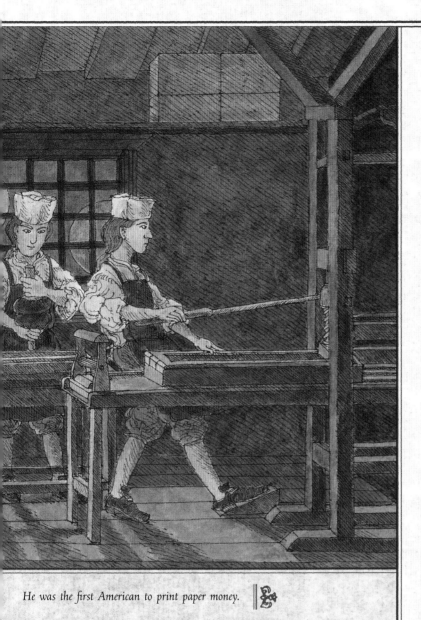

He was the first American to print paper money.

Ben and Deborah were married for forty-four years. Deborah never accompanied Ben on his trips abroad and spent all of her adult life in Philadelphia. They exchanged frequent and chatty letters. They had two children, Francis, called Franky, who died of smallpox at four, and Sarah, always known as Sally.

Other shopkeepers marveled at Franklin's energy. One observed, "I see him still at work when I go home . . . and he is at work again before his neighbors get out of bed." He was careful to be seen working hard, delivering his own supplies from the docks, always reinforcing the image of an industrious, enterprising, and frugal young man.

authority and formal affairs. He sought to promote truth and the public good, and, of course, to sell newspapers. This ability to appear neutral would later serve him well, as politician and statesman.

He wrote a famous article called "Apology for Printers." In it he defended printing opposing viewpoints on issues. Franklin said dissenting views were necessary, or the public would "have nothing to read but the opinion of printers." He loved biting gossip, usually putting it in the *Gazette* in the guise of letters he wrote and signed, "Alice Addertongue."

Ben's life would be defined by print. He signed his name, "B. Franklin, Printer." Printing made him prosperous and celebrated, and it provided him the means to political leadership. He was not a strong speaker, in an era when oratory was important to political success, and he rarely spoke in public for more than a few minutes at a time. Franklin's expertise lay in making the most of the printed page, delighting those who agreed with him, and disarming those who did not; always keeping all parties anticipating his next move.

Temperance
Silence
Order
Resolution
Frugality
Industry

Humility

Sincerity
Justice
Moderation
Cleanliness
Tranquility
Chastity

Franklin made a list of thirteen "virtues" he thought might help him develop good habits. He kept a record of his progress, and writing in his autobiography when he was in his seventies, he admitted failure with "humility."

"In reality," he said, "there is, perhaps, no one of our natural passions so hard to subdue as Pride, for even if I could conceive completely overcoming it, I should probably be proud of my humility."

IN 1732, FRANKLIN published his first *Almanack*, a slim pocket-sized book containing calendars, times of sunrises and sunsets, moon phases, weather forecasts, travel information, how-tos, and general advice. After the Bible, almanacs were the favorite book in almost all houses, the main source of information and entertainment.

Franklin's concept of an almanac was hardly new. He sold almanacs imported from England in his shop, and there were several others printed in Philadelphia when his *Poor Richard, an Almanack* appeared.

What made Franklin's almanac unique was the narrator, a made-up character named Poor Richard Saunders. He was an idle astrologer who was constantly nagged by his wife to get a "real job." Through Richard's voice, Franklin was able to express his own witty and inventive opinions on just about everything. Franklin created this distinct character who even thanked those who purchased the *Almanack* for finally providing him an income that stopped his wife's nagging. The almanac included recipes, jokes, poems, odd facts, articles on agriculture, astrology, and advice from Saunders on marriage and bachelorhood.

People bought *Poor Richard's Almanack* because of its whimsical sayings and proverbs. They were not all Franklin's original ideas; many were taken

"Everything puts me in mind of a story."

from other almanacs and earlier writings, which he shortened and rewrote to show off with his own wit and insights. "Why should I give my readers bad lines of my own," he asked, "when good ones of other people's are plenty?" He thought Poor Richard would educate its readers. "I considered it a proper vehicle," he wrote, "for conveying instruction among the common People, who bought scarce any other book."

In Poor Richard's final edition in 1758, Franklin assembled about one hundred sayings from previous issues. They are spoken by an old man called Father Abraham, who lectures a crowd on frugal and virtuous behavior. Franklin scoffingly describes the crowd's reaction to Father Abraham's sermonizing by stating, "The people heard it, and approved the doctrine, and immediately practiced the contrary." This article proved so popular that Franklin printed it in a special edition called *The Way to Wealth*. It became the best-known book in America, reprinted 145 times, and in seven languages in Europe.

Poor Richard's Almanack was the most successful publication in America. Reprinting each fall, and selling ten thousand copies annually, it was the equivalent of more than two million copies today. It was printed for twenty-five years and made Franklin's greatest fortune.

"A lie stands on one leg, the truth on two."

"An egg today is better than a hen tomorrow."

"The family of Fools is ancient."

"None preaches better than the ant, and she says nothing."

"A country man between two lawyers is like a fish between two cats."

"Early to bed, early to rise, makes a man healthy, wealthy, and wise."

Poor Richard, 1733.

AN
Almanack
For the Year of Chrift
1733,
Being the Firft after LEAP YEAR:

Wherein is contained
The Locations, Eclipfes, Judgment of
the Weather, Spring Tides, Planets Motions &
mutual Afpects, Sun and Moon's Rifing and Set-
tings, Length of Days, Time of High Water,
Fairs, Courts, and obferable Days.

The Anatomy of Man's Body as govern'd by the Twelve Confellations.

♈ The Head and Face.

ΙΙ Arms — ♌ Heart — ♎ Reins — ♐ Thigh — ♒ Legs

♉ Neck — ♋ Breaft — ♍ Bowels — ♏ Secret — ♑ Knees

♓ The Feet.

To know where the sign is.
Firft Find the Day of the Month, and againft the Day you
have the sign or Place of the Moon in the 5th Column.
Then finding the Sign here, it Fhews the Part of the Body
it governs.

The Names and Characters of the Seven Planets.
☉ Sol, ♄ Saturn, ♃ Jupiter, ♂ Mars, ♀ Venus,
☿ Mercury, ☽ Luna, ☊ Dragon's Head and ☋ Tail.

I am, Your faithful servant,
R. SAUNDERS.
1733
By *RICHARD SAUNDERS*. Philom.
PHILADELPHIA:
Printed and fold by B. Franklin, at the New
Printing-Office near the Market.

"A penny saved is a penny earned."

"Fish and visitors stink in three days."

"Who has deceiv'd thee as oft as thy self?"

"A mob's a Monster; heads enough, but no brains."

"People who are wrapped up in themselves make small packages."

"If you would know the value of money, try to borrow some."

The above design reflects the general feeling of the Almanack, and is not intended to be an accurate depiction of any actual page, in any particular volume. Many of the proverbs were illustrated with quaint images that echo the social values of Franklin's time. We often use some of these phrases in ordinary speech today without realizing they first appeared in the writings of Poor Richard.

FRANKLIN WAS a firm believer in the power of the people in the community working together for a common good. He wanted conditions to be better—for everyone, himself included. Ben also wanted to make people aware of what was wrong and get them involved in improving things for themselves. He was always coming up with ideas and persuading people to go along with them.

Ben would recognize a problem and then talk about it at his weekly gatherings. That got people's attention. Then he would write about it in his newspaper, where anyone who wanted to could read about it. He did all this in as fairminded a way as possible, because he didn't want anyone to harbor bad feelings or be jealous of him. He was a master organizer and planner, while appearing to remain in the background.

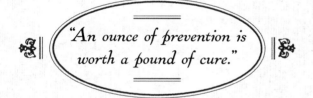

"An ounce of prevention is worth a pound of cure."

One early project of Ben's was Philadelphia's unpaved streets, choked with dust in dry weather and a muddy mess when it rained. He convinced residents to pay the city a small tax to provide street cleaners and lamplighters, and got people to ask the local governing body, called the Assembly, to begin paving the streets. Streetlights were an invention of Ben's.

He printed a pamphlet encouraging a college in Philadelphia, and raised enough money to open an academy where poor children did not have to pay. It later became the University of Pennsylvania. He started schools for Native Americans and African Americans.

Franklin was a key founder of the first hospital in America. He sponsored a police force, where townspeople paid to have their streets patrolled. He formed a volunteer fire brigade. It became

ABOVE: *A. Handheld rattle to sound alarm. B. Leather fire bucket. C. Flambeau, or night torch. D. Lantern used by fire warden.*

the nation's first full-time firefighting force.

Franklin was the city's leading printer and publisher. He was named postmaster of Philadelphia, and later of North America. In 1737, he became clerk of the Assembly. Benjamin Franklin was easily Philadelphia's most prominent citizen.

Franklin thought women should learn accounting. It was, he said, "likely to be of more use to them and their children in case of widowhood, than either music or dancing."

 Fire was a constant threat in crowded cities with many wooden buildings and no running water. Colonial firefighters formed into bucket brigades, and used leather buckets to throw water on fires or to fill a tank on a fire engine which was pumped by hand to shoot a stream of water. One line of the brigade passed full buckets of water to the pumper, while another line passed the empty buckets back to the water's source. Hook and ladder firefighters pulled down sections of the burning buildings.

Franklin became postmaster of Philadelphia in 1737. Until then, people had to pick up their own mail. He introduced home delivery, which cost a penny for each letter. He now had a way to deliver the Gazette—he sent it along with the post riders.

Franklin helped establish the first schools for African Americans. "Their apprehension seems quick," he wrote, "their memory as strong, and their docility in every respect equal to that of white children. You will wonder perhaps that I should ever doubt it . . ."

BEN FRANKLIN'S first invention may have been swim fins, when he was a boy. They were wooden paddles strapped to his hands, which he concluded did not really work all that well. But that did not discourage Ben. He was an inventor his whole life.

Ben was curious about all manner of things, and he loved to tinker. But nothing pleased him more than to think up something that had a useful purpose. He came up with designs and plans for many objects and improvements throughout his life. One of his most useful was a heating stove that we know now as the Franklin stove.

In colonial times the fireplace provided the only heat in homes, but it wasn't very efficient. Most of the heat went up the chimney, and rooms became smoky. In 1742, Franklin designed an iron stove that fit into a fireplace. When the iron sides were heated, warm air drifted out into the room, and the smoke went up the chimney. Franklin never patented the stove, which he called the Pennsylvania Fire Place. Nor did he make money from any of his inventions. He felt it was his civic duty to share anything that improved the common good of the people. "That as we enjoy great Advantages from the Inventions of others, we should be glad of an Opportunity to serve others by any Inventions of ours, and this we should do freely and generously," he said.

Franklin's method of solving a problem was straightforward and practical. He would pose a

 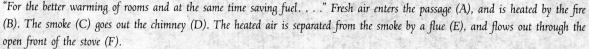 *"For the better warming of rooms and at the same time saving fuel. . . ."* Fresh air enters the passage (A), and is heated by the fire (B). The smoke (C) goes out the chimney (D). The heated air is separated from the smoke by a flue (E), and flows out through the open front of the stove (F).

 Franklin was seventy-eight when he made his Double Spectacles, "serving for distant objects as well as near ones. . . . as I wear my spectacles constantly, I have only to move my eyes up or down . . ."

question, and then experiment in a logical process of setting up equipment, observing, studying the outcome, and then making a reasoned deduction. These are the basic steps of what we call the scientific method today. This procedure was new to the eighteenth century, but it became the widely accepted way of conducting experiments.

Working until he was eighty years old, Ben invented among other things his stove, the lightning rod, odometer, a library chair (with ladder), a chair with a writing arm, a twenty-four-hour clock, a four-sided streetlamp, the armonica, bifocals, and the long-armed pole to reach objects on a high shelf.

Franklin made an odometer, an instrument he attached to the wheel of a carriage that measured miles by the number of times the wheel turned. In 1763, with his daughter, Sally, he toured the colonies as postmaster general, on a trip that took five months and covered more than 1,750 miles.

A. The long-armed pole, B. the library chair, C. the writing chair, D. the streetlamp.

The armonica had thirty-seven glass hemispheres that were turned by a foot pedal. Pressing against the turning spheres with wet fingers provided a clear, rich tone. Both Beethoven and Mozart wrote music for it.

Ben published "A Modest Inquiry into the Nature and Necessity of Paper Currency," and designed a leaf pattern that was difficult to counterfeit by pressing leaves into plaster of paris molds. In his career he printed more than two million bills.

WHEN BENJAMIN FRANKLIN was forty-two years old he was wealthy enough to retire from business. He turned his attention to "Natural Philosophy," as science was then called. Scientific exploration in his time was regarded as more of a hobby, something one might pursue part time. It was not the field it is today. Practitioners worked alone; there were no university laboratories, no government support. And scientists were basically self taught.

Franklin's drive to experiment and record observations "for the common benefit of mankind" led to his founding the American Philosophical Society in 1743, in Philadelphia. The first organization in America dedicated to science, its mission was to derive practical uses acquired through investigation of topics as diverse as physics, medicine, history, mathematics, agriculture, geology, raising farm animals, archaeology . . . "and all philosophical experiments that let light into the nature of things."

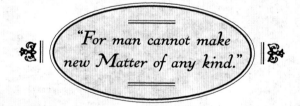

"For man cannot make new Matter of any kind."

Franklin wanted to know how everything worked. He applied the lofty goals of the Society to such ordinary concerns as variations in climate, storms, taxation, chimney construction, magnetism, why canal boats move faster in deep water than in shallow water, and improvements in juices, cider, and wine. He wrote about exercise, sunspots, lead poisoning, and the rotation of the earth.

Throughout his life, Franklin corresponded with scientists and scholars on both sides of the Atlantic. After he received an honorary degree from St. Andrew's University in Scotland, he was known and addressed internationally—and by himself—as Doctor Franklin.

Living before the discovery of germs and viruses, Franklin concluded: "Some unknown Quality in the Air may perhaps sometimes produce Colds, as in the influenza."

* * *

"I suppose the warmth generally increases with quickness of pulse," he said. He swam, climbed flights of stairs, and swung weights. Franklin made one of the earliest connections between exercise and calories of heat.

* * *

Franklin was a believer in the benefits of fresh air and took "cold air baths," sitting naked, reading for an hour or more, in a cold room. He also installed a copper tub with a shelf so he could read while taking hot baths.

52	61	4	13	20	29	36	45
14	3	62	51	46	35	30	19
53	60	5	12	21	28	37	44
11	6	59	54	43	38	27	22
55	58	7	10	23	26	39	42
9	8	57	56	41	40	25	24
50	63	2	15	18	31	34	47
16	1	64	49	48	33	32	17

Franklin made "Magic Squares" to combat boredom during debates in the Pennsylvania Assembly. Each single row, vertical or horizontal, adds up to 260. Half of each row, from the outer edge in, equals 130.

In 1783, a major volcano erupted in Iceland. Northern Europe was covered by a thick blue haze of pollution. Franklin published a paper on the "constant Fog," rightly identifying the volcano as the cause.

He observed and recorded comets, eclipses, sunspots, and the transit of Venus and Mars across the surface of the sun.

A.

Fig 4
a b c d e f g
D.
B.

C.

D.

The rotation of the Earth affects cloud and wind patterns

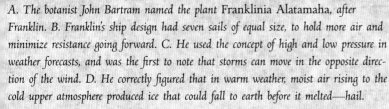

A. The botanist John Bartram named the plant Franklinia Alatamaha, after Franklin. B. Franklin's ship design had seven sails of equal size, to hold more air and minimize resistance going forward. C. He used the concept of high and low pressure in weather forecasts, and was the first to note that storms can move in the opposite direction of the wind. D. He correctly figured that in warm weather, moist air rising to the cold upper atmosphere produced ice that could fall to earth before it melted—hail.

Observing insects under a microscope led him to note "a World utterly unknown to the Ancients. Flies . . . have a great Number of eyes fix'd to their Heads, so they see on all Sides around them without turning their Heads or Eyes."

He placed different colored fabric squares on the snow. The darker colored squares sank, proof that darker colored clothing absorbs more light, and so is warmer.

Franklin knew the Gulf Stream was like a warm river floating on the ocean. He found the water much cooler below the stream, as much as 12 degrees. The warm water carried ships faster from America to England. After measuring the temperature numerous times on his many Atlantic voyages, Franklin advised that a "thermometer might be a useful instrument for a navigator."

Franklin thought the earth might have been once covered by water, since seashells were found in high places, above sea level.

THE NATURAL spectacle of lightning has always fascinated and terrified humans. The violent displays of brilliant light, the crashing peals of accompanying thunder, and the constant threat of damage from fire make this one of nature's most fearsome displays.

The ancients believed lightning to be an expression of anger and reprisal from their gods. In Greek and Roman mythology, the thunderbolt was hurled from the hands of Zeus. Even in Franklin's day, religious figures in America and Europe ranted that the ravages of lightning were punishment from God for sinful behavior. But it was at this time that curious men were just beginning to understand the fundamentals of electricity. Benjamin Franklin was one of these curious men.

Franklin became fascinated by electricity after he saw an "electrical demonstration" in Boston in 1743. In one of the tricks using static electricity, sparks came from the feet of a boy suspended from the ceiling by a silk rope.

Ben began his own experiments using a glass tube for producing static electricity that he received from his colleague in London, Peter Collinson. His first work involved studying electric charges drawn from his spinning glass tube. He had two friends charged with static electricity, and when they touched each other, the electrical charges moved back and forth between them. Ben conjectured that one person was electrified "positively," and the other person, "negatively," "terms we may use until your philosophers give us better." These terms, of course, have never been improved upon. We still use them today along with other familiar names Franklin made up, such as battery, conductor, charge, and discharge.

Franklin's most important discovery was that a positive electric charge is always accompanied by an equal negative charge. This finding, called the Law of the Conservation of Charge, is basic in all electrical science and fits well with Franklin's belief in all things being in balance.

Franklin was sure that electricity and lightning were the same thing. In 1749, he made a list of similarities between them which included "giving light, crooked direction, and conducted by metals, and a crack or noise in exploding."

Determined to prove that electricity and lightning are the same thing, he conducted his celebrated kite experiment. With his adopted son, William, he built a silk kite with two cross-sticks,

"Let the experiment be made."

Franklin's electrical work was not limited to serious study. He electrified the iron fence around his house, which provided sparks to amused visitors.

Franklin's demonstrations drew large crowds. He charged a portrait of King George II, so that "conspirators" who touched the crown received a "high treason shock."

In 1751, Franklin published "Experiments and Observations on Electricity," in London. It made his fame as a scientist in Europe. French scientists, using his information, proved clouds could hold electricity—lightning. Franklin conducted his kite experiment in June, 1752, a full month before the news from France reached America.

with a pointed wire rising one foot above the wooden sticks. At the end of the string near his hands, he fixed a silk ribbon to a key. His son got the kite aloft and they waited in a cowshed as a storm passed overhead. For some time nothing happened, and Ben was dismayed. But finally lightning struck the kite. Holding the wet string tightly he felt tension, and the strands on the string began to rise up. He knew the string was carrying a charge. He touched the key and felt the shock of an electric spark. He stored part of the charge in a water-filled Leyden jar, and discovered it was similar to electricity he created in laboratory experiments. ". . . and thereby," he wrote Collinson, "the sameness of the electric matter with

that of lightning [is] completely demonstrated."

His kite experiment and his findings on electricity made him famous in Europe. In fact, he became the most celebrated man in America.

What is this phenomenon that shoots fireballs from the sky? Lightning is the result of atmospheric bursts of electricity, which jump from one cloud to another, or between a cloud and the earth, wherever enough tension between opposite charges, positive and negative, have built up.

covered that a pointed piece of metal was a better conductor of electricity than a blunt one. He reasoned that by fixing a pointed metal rod on the highest part of a building, and running a wire from the rod down the side of the building into the ground, electricity could be drawn out of the clouds and conducted down the wire harmlessly into the earth, away from the building itself.

This was the first lightning rod, an instrument of such significance that it forever changed safety standards for buildings. "A house thus furnished will not be damaged by lightning, it being attracted by the Points, and passing thro the Metal into the Ground, without hurting any Thing."

It may be difficult for us to appreciate the calming impact this device would have had on the fearful, suspicious people of Franklin's era. John Adams, his compatriot and sometime rival, declared, "The idea [of a lightning rod] was one of the most sublime that ever entered a human imagination, that a mortal should disarm the clouds of heaven."

At first, some people were afraid to put up lightning rods. They thought their use might bring down the fury of God. But the rods were so effective against damage and fire that "Franklin's rod" soon became accepted by all. This spread his fame internationally by a far greater degree than any of his previous scientific accomplishments ever had.

Franklin always sought to master what he began, even if his study of electricity was only a "hobby." Franklin was trying to understand the nature of electrical behavior, working on his own and corresponding with a few others, mostly in Europe. He used tubelike glass containers called Leyden jars in his experiments, as shown on the opposite page. The glass jar was filled with water,

The first lightning rod was raised in Philadelphia, on the house of the painter Benjamin West, who painted a portrait of Franklin himself. The spectacle of the rod conducting electricity safely caused a sensation in 1753.

BENJAMIN FRANKLIN was both fascinated and intrigued by his study of electricity. But what *use* could he make of proving that electricity and lightning were the same thing? A practical use was the most important thing to Ben. As part of his experiments, he had already dis-

In Franklin's time, there were no science labs. For equipment people used objects they had around the house. One such object was called the Leyden jar. It was a kind of wide glass tube named after the town in Holland where it had been invented. Ben worked by himself.

and had a cork stopper with a metal rod projecting down into the water. The jar was coated inside and out with metal foil. When the jar was electrically charged, it gave off a strong shock when touched (A). Franklin wanted to know what held such a volume of electricity—the metal rod, the water, the glass, or some combination? He removed the rod and the jar still gave a strong spark (B). He removed the water into a separate jar, but the water gave no spark (C). The empty Leyden jar still gave a shock. The electric charge was held in the jar alone (D). When he tested the glass without metal foil, the glass remained charged. But the metal foil gave no charge (E). So Franklin concluded, "The whole force and power of giving a shock is in the glass itself."

He used the terms "charge" and "discharge" in describing the experiment. "So wonderfully are the two States of Electricity, the plus and minus combined and balanced in this miraculous Bottle!" Franklin had discovered the principle of the electrical condenser, a mechanism eventually used in radios, televisions, and telephone circuits. At the time, his extraordinary findings about electricity were noted by like-minded scientists, but their importance in the future would be monumental.

Franklin's "Electrical Battery" consisted of rows of Leyden jars linked together to store a greater amount of electricity.

Trying to electrocute a turkey for a dinner party, he touched two wires at once and was knocked senseless. "I am ashamed," he wrote, "to have been guilty of so notorious a blunder." And he added, "I meant to kill a turkey, and instead, I nearly killed a goose."

ENGLAND WAS not the only European country with outposts in the New World. France was also eager to expand its territory there. England's enemy in Europe, France enlisted the Native Americans to their side to fight against the British in America.

Relations between Native Americans and European settlers in and around Philadelphia had been relatively peaceful since the treaty between William Penn—the founder of Pennsylvania—and the Lenape tribe, in 1682. But by 1747, wars for territory between the British soldiers and the French and their Indian allies in western Pennsylvania posed a threat to Philadelphia and eastern areas.

Franklin, in a pamphlet "Plain Truth," called for forming a militia for defense. This was a radical idea—the Quakers were opposed to the military, and it was an admission that the British troops were not able to protect citizens. Franklin raised a force of 10,000 men, and a lottery was held to get arms and ammunition. The militia was made up of ordinary civilians Franklin called "the middling people."

Even so, these French and Indian Wars esca-lated, and in 1754, Franklin was asked by colonial delegates to broker a treaty between British colonies and the Six Nations of the Iroquois. This was an attempt to keep these tribes from siding with the French. Colonial delegates and Iroquois met in Albany, New York, where Franklin sponsored a Plan of Union for mutual defense and solidarity.

Franklin was impressed with the dignity shown by the chiefs of the Six Nations of the Iroquois Federation. He was also impressed with the tribes' basic concept of peace, justice, and respect for the "power of the good words," the knowledge of the elders. He thought the colonists could learn something about organization from the Iroquois belief in tribal unity and unanimous consent.

The Iroquois and the delegates approved the plan, but it was rejected by the English king as too democratic. The plan, however, never had any intention of renouncing any British colonial control. The plan was also rejected by every colony as giving too much power to a central government. Franklin always felt this treaty might have prevented the Revolution.

Colonial taxpayers paid for their own militia

 "Colonel" Franklin, supervising the construction of a fort as commander of the militia. "I undertook this military Business, tho' I didn't conceive myself well qualified for it." Franklin spent his fiftieth birthday with his men, sleeping in a snow-covered barn.

Franklin's early opinions of Native Americans were as prejudiced as most colonists'. To the new settlers, the Indians appeared bizarre and uncivilized. As he came into more frequent contact with them, Franklin's views began to change. He admired their manner of negotiating. At Albany, Franklin was taken by the Iroquois policy of not commenting on a proposal until the next day. Sometimes treaties between "civilized" white men and native peoples were not honored. Franklin believed most problems between colonists and Indians were caused "by some injustice" on the part of the white settlers.

protection, but Pennsylvania's largest land owners, the Penn family, paid nothing. Franklin, acting as agent for Pennsylvania, sailed to London in 1757 to persuade Parliament to force the Penns to pay their share. This trip was one of three that Franklin made to Europe as representative of the colonists. It took over three years to reach a rea-

sonable compromise. Franklin returned home in 1762, with more knowledge of the world but still a strong believer in colonial ties to England.

Franklin and other colonial leaders were curious about their environment, but not because they wanted to preserve it. They were mostly interested in what economic value this vast land might hold for them. They wanted to tame the wilderness, settle people there, and put it to use. Franklin's interest favored machines and industry; in the South, the emphasis was on farming. America became a rich nation from the development of its wilderness.

Franklin drew and printed the first political cartoon in America, May 9, 1754, in the Gazette. The image illustrated his desire for the colonies to unite against French and Indian incursions.

THE FRENCH AND INDIAN WARS in North America ended in 1763 with England victorious, but broke. The French were driven out of Canada. But waging war here and in Europe had been expensive. Advisers to King George recommended that American colonists be taxed to pay for the war and for keeping British soldiers in the colonies to protect against Indian attacks. The British taxes angered the colonists. "No taxation without representation" became their ringing cry. And it prompted a call for colonial representation in Parliament.

Ben Franklin was deemed the best person to represent the colonists, and he was sent to London in 1764 with a proposal for representation (as well as agent for Pennsylvania, still disputing matters with the Penns). "If you choose to tax us," he urged, "give us members in your legislature, and let us be one people." Parliament's response was the Stamp Act; it required colonists to pay a tax on every piece of printed paper,

such as newspapers and legal documents, they bought. The money went back to Britain.

The Stamp Act met with great resistance in the colonies. The colonies sent no representatives

MAD TOM.
or the MAN of RIGHTS

In January 1774, newly arrived from London, an Englishman Thomas Paine published the pamphlet "Common Sense." The pamphlet had no author listed. It became immensely popular and may have been the strongest contributor to a call for independence. "Everything that is right or natural pleads for separation," it said. Many thought Franklin was the author.

LEFT: *The Boston Tea Party. In 1773, dressed as Mohawk Indians, citizens protesting the British tax on tea dumped three shiploads of tea worth £10,000 in Boston Harbor.*

in 1768, that ". . . no middle doctrine can be well maintained," and there were only two options: "that Parliament has a power to make all laws for us, or that it has the power to make no laws for us."

In 1770, a confrontation over the new taxes erupted in Boston. British soldiers fired into a mob and killed five citizens. This event became known as the Boston Massacre. News of it spread quickly, increasing anti-British sentiment throughout the colonies. In 1771, Parliament repealed all taxes on imports except on tea. "It is not the sum paid in duty on tea that is complained of as a burden," Franklin remarked, "but the principle of the act." Things had gone too far. The Continental Congress, meeting in Philadelphia in 1774, declared that Britain had no right to govern the colonies.

Up to this point, Franklin thought the differences between the two countries could be resolved. But as he prepared to return to America, he realized that the two sides had moved even further apart. He had left America hoping for resolution. He returned believing in separation.

to Parliament, and therefore had no influence over what taxes were raised, how they were levied, or how they would be spent. Many colonists considered it a violation of their *rights as Englishmen* to be taxed without their consent—consent that only the colonial legislatures could grant.

Colonists were outraged, but Franklin took a neutral position, not wishing to anger Parliament, but seriously misreading the resentment back home. He was a believer in conciliation, but he eventually opposed the Stamp Act tax. In 1766, in an address to Parliament, he strongly influenced its repeal of the Act. Franklin had now become America's most important voice and effective spokesman.

Though the Stamp Act was repealed, this was not the end of the tax Britain wanted to collect from the colonies. Unrest in America continued over new taxes and the presence of British troops and ships in the harbors. The radical Sons of Liberty formed in Massachusetts. Franklin stated

In his final public appearance in London, in January 1774, Franklin was called before the king's Privy Council and accused of stirring unrest in the colonies. His positions as agent and colonial postmaster were revoked. He was attacked and humiliated for four hours, standing and remaining silent. He felt he was being treated like an apprentice, not a sixty-seven-year-old statesman. It was time to go home.

The Battle of Lexington in Massachusetts began April 18, 1775, when Americans fired on British marines who had ordered, "Disperse, ye rebels!"

𝓑ENJAMIN FRANKLIN had been in England for eighteen years with only a short trip back to America during that time. His mission to bring the two sides together had failed, despite his skills at arguing and influencing people. In fact, the first battle of the American Revolution took place before his ship had landed.

It was war. Franklin arrived in Philadelphia to news that American and British troops had fought in Lexington, Massachusetts. He was home only one day when he was chosen to represent Pennsylvania in the Second Continental Congress to be held in Philadelphia that May. It had now become the main city in the colonies.

Soldiers drilled in the city's streets, and in June, George Washington was appointed to lead the Continental Army against British soldiers already in the colonies.

> *"There never was a good war or a bad peace."*

Boston harbor was blockaded, and nearby the Battle of Bunker Hill was fought with heavy British losses. Franklin wrote of British actions: "You can imagine what it has done to the general temper here, which is now little short of madness."

The colonies were in rebellion. Franklin had tried to avoid war, but since the British continued in their stubborn ways, he now urged Americans to fight, even with bows and arrows if there wasn't enough gunpowder to go around.

His wife, Deborah, had died while he was in England. Now in his late sixties, Ben was still needed by the government and offered to do what he could to help. Everyone knew that he was very good at convincing people to take action. So Franklin traveled through severe winter weather to Montreal, in an unsuccessful attempt to enlist Canada in America's cause.

The Liberty Bell was made in London and hung in the Pennsylvania statehouse (now Independence Hall) in 1753. It weighed 2,080 pounds. The bell did not ring July 4, 1776, but on July 8, when the Declaration of Independence was first read to the public.

bution was making changes to tone down the language. The delegates voted to declare independence on July 2nd, and Congress approved it July 4th, 1776, the birthday of the United States of America. The delegates then signed it. Benjamin Franklin—then seventy—was the oldest. At this point Franklin was said to have quipped: "Gentlemen, we must all hang together, or most assuredly, we should all hang separately."

The British had ships with thirteen thousand sailors controlling New York harbor. The British General Howe commanded thirty thousand soldiers already there. The British quickly captured the city. The war would be difficult—farmers and tradesmen opposing the strongest nation on earth.

As for how other European powers would respond to appeals for aid, the French were interested in anything that would undermine England. But they would do little until America was officially independent.

In June of 1776, Congress called for a resolution stating: "These colonies are, and of right ought to be, free and independent states." Franklin was asked to join the committee to draw up a declaration of independence. Thomas Jefferson wrote the first draft. Franklin's major contri-

Franklin finally decided to embrace independence because of belligerent British conduct, but he was a true believer in a new kind of country and people. He had seen enough of the aristocratic framework of Europe, and supported a society where anyone could achieve success.

Benjamin Franklin, Thomas Jefferson, John Adams, Roger Sherman, and Robert Livingston met to draft the Declaration of Independence. "I wish I had written it myself," Franklin noted. Jefferson had written, "We hold these truths to be sacred and undeniable," in his draft. Franklin changed the wording to, "We hold these truths to be self-evident," deeming this more logical.

AMERICA'S position was fragile, so Franklin was sent to France to seek support for the fledgling nation. He was by far the best-known American anywhere in the world—and the most persuasive. In 1776, when he went to France, he was seventy, which was considered *very* old for the time. This was to be his last trip to Europe. The crossing was rough and cold, and Franklin was sick most of the voyage. Ben arrived in Paris to great fanfare. Despite his enormous popularity, progress was slow in getting the French to fully back America. The French were hesitant to commit until they felt America could succeed in the Revolution. One of Franklin's chief duties was to provide a positive account of the war in the colonies, but there was little change for almost two years.

Meanwhile, Franklin lived very well in a rent-free chateau between Paris and Versailles, with lavish gardens, servants, carriages, and a large wine cellar. He entertained and associated with the high society of Paris, charming everyone he felt could help further his cause with his wit and storytelling. Some Americans resented Franklin's lifestyle, particularly John Adams, who was sent to help Ben with negotiations. Adams openly disagreed with Franklin's public behavior, work ethic, and his lavish living. Adams was so abrasive the French Minister, Count Vergennes, finally refused to see him.

Franklin, however, captivated the French and kept his carefully conceived image highly visible. He made sure to appear as the wise, but ordinary man from the New World, dressing in a simple suit and fur hat, in direct contrast to the fashionable culture of nobility around him.

Jefferson said of Franklin's conversational strategy, "One of the rules that made Dr. Frank-

> *"My face is as well known as that of the man in the moon."*

On September 3, 1783, Benjamin Franklin, John Jay, and John Adams signed the Treaty of Paris, with England recognizing the United States as a free and independent nation. It established the borders from the Atlantic Ocean to the Mississippi River. east to west, and from Canada to Florida, north to south.

lin one of the most amiable men in society was never to contradict anybody." Franklin himself said, "The wit of conversation consists more in finding it in others, than showing a great deal yourself."

In December, 1777, Franklin got the break he needed. News of the American victory at Saratoga, where General Burgoyne surrendered his entire army, reached France. Paris celebrated as though the triumph was French. Negotiations moved quickly, and in March, 1778, Franklin

was received by King Louis XVI at the Palace of Versailles. A French-American treaty was signed—the first recognition of America as a nation by a world power.

Franklin had achieved a stunning diplomatic success. The Revolutionary War lasted three more years, but in October of 1781, British General Cornwallis surrendered his army, about one-fourth of Britain's forces in America, to General Washington at Yorktown, Virginia. The new nation had achieved its independence.

On the voyage to France, Franklin took two grandsons, two angora cats, and two tons of luggage. A trip could take six to eight weeks. Franklin crossed the Atlantic Ocean eight times.

Franklin witnessed the first manned balloon flight from a carriage in Paris. He was asked to sign a certificate of the flight by the balloon's designers, the Montgolfier brothers.

Franklin's reputation as a scientist raised fears in England that he would stretch a chain across the Channel and "shock" Britain with one of his electrical machines.

Franklin wrote to his daughter, Sally, that he regretted the choice of the bald eagle, "as the Representative of our Country; he is a bird of bad moral character . . . the Turk'y is in comparison a much more respectable Bird."

*N*OW THAT THE WAR WAS WON, it was time to draw up a peace treaty between the newly independent colonies and their former ruler, Britain. Franklin used all his skill in brokering agreements with the two powerful European rivals. He achieved peace with England and a continued alliance with France.

Franklin was seventy-nine, and weak, suffering from gout and kidney stones. Thomas Jefferson had come to Paris as the new American representative, and Franklin was finally going home. He left Paris to a tumultuous celebration in July of 1785, and arrived in Philadelphia in September, to an equally triumphant reception.

Shortly after arriving he was elected president of Pennsylvania. The new American government was based on the Articles of Confederation the states had agreed to in 1775, but it was working poorly. In 1787, the states agreed to meet in Philadelphia to form a stronger central government. Franklin was one of fifty-five delegates from twelve states; Rhode Island did not participate.

James Madison proposed a new concept, consisting of three equal branches of government: executive, legislative, and judicial. He also proposed a system of checks and balances so that no group could gain control and rule exclusively.

In the legislative branch, the smaller states were fearful of domination by larger states if the representation was to be by population. Franklin suggested the Grand Compromise that settled

RIGHT: *Benjamin Franklin was the only founding father to sign all three documents that created the United States of America: the Declaration of Independence (1776), the Treaty of Peace with England (1783), and the Constitution (1787).*

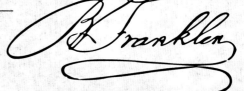

Franklin arrived in Philadelphia to adoring crowds, cannon salutes, and bells ringing. He was frail and had to be carried in a sedan chair.

The delegates worked for four months writing the Constitution, from May to September, in 1787. That summer was unusually hot, and many members enjoyed the shade of Franklin's mulberry tree. His home was close to the statehouse.

the matter. The Senate would have an equal number from each state—two—and in the House of Representatives, the number of members would be figured by population. Today, this is still the basic structure of the legislative branch.

The most difficult issue to resolve was the question of slavery. Almost half of the delegates owned slaves, and Franklin knew there would be no unified Constitution without compromise. The final settlement allowed the Southern states to retain slavery, counting a slave 3/5 of a person in the population for a state's representation in Congress. Slavery was prohibited north of the Ohio River. The vote did not approve of slavery, but certainly accepted it. The issue of ending slavery was not raised in the convention. Madison wrote that "any allusion to the subject . . . would have been a spark for a mass of gunpowder." The institution of slavery in America would last for eighty-seven more years.

Franklin's speech imploring the delegates to sign unanimously had a powerful effect. He called for an end to petty, selfish, regional interests. "From such an assembly can a perfect production be expected?" he asked. Then he added, "It therefore astonishes me, sir, to find this system so near to perfection as it does . . ." He pleaded, "that for the sake of our posterity, we shall act heartily and unanimously."

Fearing a monarchy, Franklin introduced a motion calling for three presidents, and that they should serve without pay. He was defeated on both points.

The words slave, slavery, Negroes, and Africa never appeared in the original Constitution.

ENJAMIN FRANKLIN'S final position as a public servant was as president of the Pennsylvania Society for the Abolition of Slavery. This was a Quaker group that believed it was hypocrisy to allow slavery in a society that proclaimed "all men are created free and equal." His last political act was to petition Congress, when he was eighty-three years old, to abolish slavery and the slave trade. He called for Congress to "devise means for removing the Inconsistency from the Character of the American People," and to "promote mercy and justice toward this distressed Race." Congress did not adopt this resolution, fearing the reaction of the slave-holding states.

Franklin did not always hold this conviction. He had owned slaves himself, as household servants, and his early views on slavery probably mirrored the views of most colonists—slavery was simply a fact of life. But he was an advocate of education for African Americans and Native Americans, and financially supported schools for both groups.

Franklin had envisioned the colonies becoming the center of a thriving British empire, with large productive land areas, and an expanding population with the promise of great exports. He had never intended to see the colonies separate from England. He initially even opposed non-British European immigration.

Only after the realization that England was not going to treat colonial citizens as equal British subjects, and that independence was inevitable, did he also begin to think of the issue of freedom and self-reliance for all Americans. He came to the conclusion that there could be no slavery in a new country that championed liberty and equality.

Benjamin Franklin spent his last months in his house on Market Street confined to bed, in considerable pain from kidney stones. He received visitors and wrote letters, the last one to Thomas Jefferson.

Franklin died April 17, 1790, at 11:00 in the evening, peacefully, with his family around him. His funeral, at Christ's Church, drew 20,000 people, the largest assembly ever at this time, in Philadelphia.

In his will Franklin created a trust fund for apprentice artisans in Boston and Philadelphia designed to assist them in starting new businesses. He donated his salary as president of Pennsylvania, and the fund still exists today.

of nation; one not perfect, but conceived with more respect for social and economic freedom, and concern for the rights of the individual, than any government yet devised.

Benjamin Franklin was the ideal representative of the Age of Enlightenment, a time in our history when new philosophies were emerging that rejected rigid ancient beliefs and superstition, and that championed exploration based on observation and experimentation. He was a craftsman and scientist, a writer and humorist, an inventor, a civil servant and politician, and perhaps above all a compromising thinker. He became his new nation's first diplomat and its most celebrated citizen and was acknowledged and revered as much as any individual, anywhere, living in his time.

Inherited birthright and aristocracy would have no place in his vision of America. The thirteen separate states would have no real power in the national government. He did not believe in excessive individual property holding, nor in the authority the presidency carries today. The new land would be built on the strength of free farmers, tradesmen, and shopkeepers—his beloved "middling people." Slavery was a contradictory concept.

Of all his accomplishments and gifts, Franklin's greatest may have been his untiring effort as mediator and guiding spirit in the development of the law-making process that governs the United States. His calming presence had a profound influence on the delegates, many half his age or younger.

He lived to see the creation of a new kind

His tombstone reads simply:

BENJAMIN }
And   } FRANKLIN
DEBORAH }
1790

BEN WRITES ABOUT BEN

When he was sixty-five years old (which was *very* old for someone in the 1700s), Benjamin Franklin began to write the story of his own life, called *The Autobiography of Benjamin Franklin*. He began it simply to tell his son William about his life. He never finished the book which ends well before the years of the American Revolution. It is from this book that we know so much about Ben's childhood and his life as a young man.

No book about Ben would be complete without at least a mention of his autobiography. It is a very famous book in American history not only because it tells the story of such a celebrated man. It also reflects what was important to him and how he wanted to be seen by others: that he was a hard-working, self-made businessman; that he continually looked for ways to make life better, not just for himself; and that he tried—and often failed—to live up to the virtues he espoused; and that he believed in a new kind of society built upon principles where success such as his could be obtained.

I WRITE ABOUT BEN

With a figure as famous as Franklin, there is an abundance of information about his life. I wasn't going to discover anything about him that wasn't already known, so I had to pick and choose what I thought was informative and visually interesting. I tried to present events in Franklin's life in the most intriguing, yet respectful, way, and also providing excitement and graphic variation with each page turn.

Franklin's life was so exceptional and long-lived that many incidents had to be left out in a volume of this size. I also tried to be evenhanded in recording what I thought important, and what I thought Dr. Franklin himself might have considered worthy of telling. He was not a shy man in recalling his undertakings, but he wasn't an especially boastful man either; after all his quest was always for a moderate position, if possible. I wanted to show his many sides without focusing too much on any particular one.

Finally, my intent was to give young readers a picture of what it might be like to have lived in the eighteenth century, and to better know one of its most worthy and enlightened citizens.

ABOUT THE PICTURES

When I began thinking about Benjamin Franklin and his times, I had a preconceived image of the colonial period palette being rather drab and uninteresting. A little research proved any apprehension unnecessary. Colonial colors were primarily based on natural, organic pigments, and could be rich and varied. Deep reds, purples, blues, and gold dyes were used on men's clothing (witness the famous oval portrait by J. S. Duplessis, with Ben resplendent in a red, fur-collared, three-piece suit). Women's colors were even brighter with dresses and gowns of luminous shades of pinks, greens, yellows, and violet. The interior paints and wallpaper patterns are surprisingly decorative and vivid. The homes on Elfreth's Alley, Philadelphia's oldest intact street, still use bright colors on their trim and doorways.

Franklin led a long rich life, and I wanted to picture him in as many stages of it as I could. People tend to think of him older, balding and somewhat portly, (he did refer to himself later in life as "Dr. Fatsides"), but he was fit and vigorous in his youth. Printing was no lightweight vocation. He was a strong swimmer and an advocate of physical exercise, and reputed to be a leader of his boyhood friends.

It is difficult to get a completely accurate picture of anyone living in Franklin's era. The artist must rely on prints and paintings from the period, and many of these are not necessarily reliable. No one today knows what young Ben looked like. Even likenesses after he achieved fame vary greatly. I had to assess the information available and make decisions about what to use, and how to combine things pictorially from these different sources.

Ships, buildings, costumes, and events are fairly easy to document, but the challenge lies in forming a picture that tells a specific story. The interaction of a society and its individuals must be imagined—thought out as it possibly may have taken place.

All of the artifacts, from printing presses to military uniforms, have to be depicted as correctly as possible. With Franklin's scientific experiments I combined historical images and my own improvisation. The scene with Ben at the court of Versailles is one example of just how complex the construction of a picture can be.

1706 Born in Boston to Josiah and Abiah Folger Franklin—he is their youngest son

1715 Completes his formal schooling

1717 Begins reading books voraciously, including Plutarch and Defoe. Invents the first pair of swim fins.

1718 Begins his apprenticeship to his brother James, a printer

1721 James Franklin begins publishing the *New England Courant.*

1722 Publishes for the first time under the pseudonym of Silence Dogood

1723 Takes over the *New England Courant* after James is jailed. Runs away from his apprenticeship to Philadelphia. Meets Deborah Read for the first time.

1724 Encouraged by Pennsylvania Governor William Keith, travels abroad to buy printing equipment

1725 Publishes his first pamphlet, "A Dissertation upon Liberty and Necessity, Pleasure and Pain"

1726 Returns to Philadelphia. Begins his self-improvement process by developing the thirteen virtues.

1727 Rehired by Samuel Keimer, and soon becomes supervisor of the print shop. Helps to establish the Leather Apron Club, later called the Junto.

1728 Ben Franklin and Hugh Meredith quit Keimer's print shop and set up their own.

1729 Buys the *Pennsylvania Gazette* from Samuel Keimer. Birth of William Franklin, Ben's illegitimate son whom he adopted.

1730 Elected the official printer for Pennsylvania. Marries Deborah on September 1. Buys Hugh Meredith's share of their business, getting full control of their print shop and the *Pennsylvania Gazette*. Argues for fire protection programs after a fire destroys the southern part of Philadelphia.

1731 Creates the Library Company of Philadelphia—the first lending library in the country

1732 Birth of his son Francis Folger Franklin. Publishes the first edition of *Poor Richard's Almanack.*

1736 Named clerk of the Pennsylvania Assembly. Prints currency for New Jersey. Son Francis Folger dies at age four of smallpox. Creates the Union Fire Company, one of the first American volunteer-based firefighting companies.

1737 Chosen as postmaster of Philadelphia

1740 Becomes the official printer for New Jersey

1741 Publishes *The General Magazine and Historical Chronicle,* one of America's first magazines

1742 Sponsors and publicizes plant-collecting trips by John Bartram, a renowned Philadelphia botanist

1743 Attends Archibald Spencer's lectures in Boston on natural philosophy. Electricity is discussed. Birth of his daughter, Sarah Franklin.

1744 The American Philosophical Society begins meeting. Invents the Franklin Stove, otherwise known as the Pennsylvania Fireplace.

1746 Begins experimenting with electricity

1747 Organizes Philadelphia militia

1749 Appointed president of the Academy and College of Philadelphia

1750 Invents the lightning rod. Begins planning the Pennsylvania Hospital, which will provide care to the poor and mentally unwell.

1751 Letters on electricity published by Peter Collinson in London

1752 Conducts famous kite experiment. Helps create the first American mutual fire insurance company.

1753 Harvard and Yale award Franklin honorary degrees. Declared joint deputy postmaster general of North America. Awarded the Royal Society's Copley Medal for his work with electricity.

1754 Publishes the first American political cartoon in the *Pennsylvania Gazette*, entitled Join or Die. Proposes plans for colonial union at Albany congress.

1755 Construction began on the Pennsylvania Hospital.

1757 Leaves for England as representative for Georgia, Massachusetts, New Jersey, and Pennsylvania

1758 The final edition of *Poor Richard's Almanack* is published. Publishes *The Way to Wealth.*

1759 The University of St. Andrews, Scotland, awards Franklin an honorary degree of Doctor of Laws.

1762 Invents glass armonica

1763 Returns to the colonies from abroad

1764–65 Charts the course of the Gulf Stream

1766 Supports the repeal of the Stamp Act in the House of Commons. Elected to join the Royal Society of Sciences.

1771 Begins writing his autobiography

1774 Deborah Read dies of a stroke while Franklin is abroad.

1775 Elected as a Pennsylvania delegate to second Continental Congress. Elected postmaster general of the colonies.

1776 Supervises the Constitutional Convention of Pennsylvania. Helps draft and signs the Declaration of Independence. Arrives in Paris as a colonial ambassador to the French Court.

1778 Succeeds in obtaining French aid and alliance in the Revolutionary War

1783 Signs the Treaty of Paris, along with John Adams and John Jay

1784 Invents bifocals

1785 Elected president of Pennsylvania executive council

1787 Signs the United States Constitution at the Constitutional Convention. Becomes president of the Society for the Abolition of Slavery.

1790 Dies of pleurisy in Philadelphia on April 17, at the age of eighty-four

BIBLIOGRAPHY

Bowen, Catherine Drinker. *The Most Dangerous Man in America*. Boston: Little Brown & Co., 1974.

Dray, Philip. *Stealing God's Thunder*. New York: Random House, 2005.

Franklin, Benjamin. *The Autobiography of Benjamin Franklin*. Many editions.

—. *Poor Richard's Almanack*. Many editons.

Goodman, Nathan, ed. *A Benjamin Franklin Reader*. New York: Thomas Y. Crowell Company, 1945.

Issacson, Walter. *Benjamin Franklin, An American Life*. New York: Simon and Schuster, 2004.

Morgan, Edmund S., ed. *Not Your Usual Founding Father*. New Haven: Yale University Press, 2006.

Talbott, Page, ed. *Benjamin Franklin: In Search of a Better World*. New Haven: Yale University Press, 2005.

Van Doren, Carl. *Benjamin Franklin*. New York: Viking Press, 1938.

Wood, Gordon S. *The Americanization of Benjamin Franklin*. New York: The Penguin Press, 2004.

FOR YOUNG READERS

Adler. David A. *B. Franklin, Printer*. New York: Holiday House, 2001.

Aliki. *The Many Lives of Benjamin Franklin*. Englewood Cliffs, NJ: Prentice-Hall Inc., 1977.

Fritz, Jean. *What's the Big Idea, Ben Franklin?* New York: Penguin Books for Young Readers, 1976.

Giblin, James Cross. *The Amazing Life of Benjamin Franklin*. New York: Scholastic Press, 2000.

Greene, Carol. *Benjamin Franklin, A Man with Many Jobs*. Chicago: Children's Press, 1988.

Meltzer, Milton. *Benjamin Franklin, the New American*. New York: Franklin Watts, 1988.

Schanzer, Rosalyn. *How Benjamin Franklin Stole the Lightning*. New York: Harper Collins, 2003.

Stewart, Gail B. *The Importance of Benjamin Franklin*. San Deigo, CA: Lucent Books Inc., 1992.

IMPORTANT VISUAL SOURCES FOR THE ILLUSTRATIONS

The Library of the Franklin Institute, 222 N. 20th St., Philadelphia, PA 19103

Country Beautiful, eds. "The Most Amazing Benjamin Franklin." Waukesha, WI: *Country Beautiful*, 1973.

Fleming, Thomas. *Liberty! The American Revolution*. New York: The Viking Press, 1997.

Looney, Robert F. *Old Philadelphia in Early Photographs 1839–1914*. New York: Dover Books, 1976.

Racinet, Auguste. *Racinet's Full-Color Pictorial History of Western Costume*. New York: Dover Books, 1987.

Tunis, Edwin. *Colonial Living*. New York: The World Publishing Company, 1957.

—. *Oars, Sails, and Steam*. New York: Thomas Y. Crowell, 1952.

THE HIGHLIGHTED QUOTATIONS THAT APPEAR IN LARGE TYPE IN THE BOOK ARE TAKEN FROM BENJAMIN FRANKLIN'S WRITINGS. MOST ARE FROM HIS AUTOBIOGRAPHY, BUT OTHERS ARE FROM LETTERS, HIS ALMANACS, AND OTHER OFFICIAL PAPERS.

To Jennifer, Rob, and Anne-Marie

DIAL BOOKS FOR YOUNG READERS

A division of Penguin Young Readers Group

PUBLISHED BY THE PENGUIN GROUP

Penguin Group (USA) Inc., 375 Hudson Street, New York, New York 10014, U.S.A. • Penguin Group (Canada), 90 Eglinton Avenue East, Suite 700, Toronto, Ontario, Canada M4P 2Y3 (a division of Pearson Penguin Canada Inc.) • Penguin Books Ltd, 80 Strand, London WC2R 0RL, England • Penguin Ireland, 25 St Stephen's Green, Dublin 2, Ireland (a division of Penguin Books Ltd) • Penguin Group (Australia), 250 Camberwell Road, Camberwell, Victoria 3124, Australia (a division of Pearson Australia Group Pty Ltd) • Penguin Books India Pvt Ltd, 11 Community Centre, Panchsheel Park, New Delhi—110 017, India • Penguin Group (NZ), 67 Apollo Drive, Rosedale, Auckland 0632, New Zealand (a division of Pearson New Zealand Ltd) • Penguin Books (South Africa) (Pty) Ltd, 24 Sturdee Avenue, Rosebank, Johannesburg 2196, South Africa • Penguin Books Ltd, Registered Offices: 80 Strand, London WC2R 0RL, England

Library of Congress Cataloging-in-Publication Data

Byrd, Robert.

Electric Ben : the amazing life and times of Benjamin Franklin / by Robert Byrd.

p. cm.

Dial Books for Young Readers.

ISBN 978-0-8037-3749-5 (hardcover)

1. Franklin, Benjamin, 1706–1790—Juvenile literature. 2. Statesmen—United States—Biography—Juvenile literature. 3. Inventors—United States—Biography—Juvenile literature. 4. Scientists—United States—Biography—Juvenile literature. 5. Printers—United States—Biography—Juvenile literature. I. Title.

E302.6.F8B97 2012

973.3092—dc23

[B] 2011050493

Published in the United States by Dial Books for Young Readers, a division of Penguin Young Readers Group

345 Hudson Street, New York, New York 10014 • www.penguin.com/youngreaders

The artwork for this book was created using ink-line, watercolor, and colored inks on 140 lb. coldpress Arches watercolor paper.

Designed by Jason Henry

Manufactured in the U.S.A. • First Edition

5 7 9 10 8 6

ALWAYS LEARNING   **PEARSON**

A TRUE FRIEND IS
THE BEST POSSESSION.

HOW FEW THER[E] [ARE THAT H]AVE COURAGE ENOUGH TO OWN THEIR FAULTS, OR RESOLUTION ENOUGH TO MEND THEM! ———

NO GA[INS WIT]HOUT PAINS.

RICHES ARE REALLY AND TRULY OF NO GREAT USE; A RIGHT HEART EXCEEDS ALL.

OF LEARNED FOOLS I HAVE SEEN TEN TIMES TEN, OF UNLEARNED WISE MEN I HAVE SEEN A HUNDRED. ———

HE THAT SOWS THORNS, SHOULD NOT GO BAREFOOT. ———

LOVE, AND BE LOV'D. ———

BEWARE OF LITTLE EXPENSES, A SMALL LEAK WILL SINK A GREAT SHIP. ———

BE NEITHER SILLY, NOR CUNNING, BUT WISE. ———

ARE YOU ANGRY THAT OTHERS DISAPPOINT YOU? REMEMBER YOU CANNOT DEPEND UPON YOURSELF.

NEITHER A BORROWER NOR A LENDER BE.

POVERTY WANTS SOME THINGS, LUXURY MANY THINGS, AVARICE ALL THINGS. ———

THE SUN NEVER REPENTS OF THE GOOD HE DOES, NOR DOES HE EVER DEMAND A RECOMPENCE. ———

EAT TO LIVE, AND NOT LIVE TO EAT.

BETTER SLIP WITH FOOT THAN TONGUE. ———